Amicable Numbers

Mike Barlow

D1341038

Templar Poetry

First Published 2008 by Templar Poetry
Templar Poetry is an imprint of Delamide & Bell

Fenelon House,
Kingsbridge Terrace
Dale Road, Matlock, Derbyshire
DE4 3NB

www.templarpoetry.co.uk

ISBN 978-1-906285-27-2

A CIP catalogue record for this book is available from the British Library.

For permission to reprint or broadcast these poems write to
Templar Poetry

Typeset by Pliny
Graphics by Paloma Violet
Printed and bound in Turkey

Also by the Author

Living on the Difference
(Smiths Doorstop)

Another Place
(Salt)

Acknowledgements

Versions of some of these poems have appeared in the following magazines: *Dreamcatcher, Interpreter's House, Poetry Nottingham, The Rialto, Seam, Smiths Knoll and Staple.*

ARTS COUNCIL ENGLAND

Contents

Twenty Something Going On Immortal

I've just stepped onto the overhanging rib.
Beneath me is space and a ribbon of road
that could be a slight blemish on the print.
I'm looking upwards, leaning out slightly
to get an idea of the moves ahead,
the brackets of my arms look firm,
one hand's on a perfect jug, the other
flat against the wall, the toes of my boots
bend on tiny ledges. If a leg shakes you can't see.
Nor can you sense the dry mouth,
the taut nexus of muscles. From my waist
the rope loops towards my second.
She's belayed on an airy ledge, paying out
and watching. What we commit
to one another's care up here's not spoken of.
It's no more than a few seconds
before I reach up, aware only of the space beneath,
the game of holds, the improbability of it all.

When I've gone the same piece of rock rib
will jut against the sky, and a line of rope
mark out a sequence of inevitable moves.

A First Anniversary

She's outside the back door
lighting a paper nest in a metal bin.
She feeds it from a shoe-box –
letters, photos, tickets for a Dylan concert,
labels from Amsterdam, Prague.
Now and then a name takes flight,
quickens the blood. Her head rings
through to Paris, that accent, clear
as next door, catching her off-guard;
round her shoulders an old blue pullover
she fancies still smells of its original wearer.

When her yearling husband finds her
she's a wraith, mobbed by ash grey wings,
the tree by the water trough hung
with paper crows. Embers nibble her hair.
A photo glides to the ground,
a green-edged grin of flame
eating its way towards someone's eyes.
Not understanding, he tries to help,
pounces, pokes it back,
not understanding again
when she goes indoors, leaves him to it.

Out Of My Body

God knows who put what in my drink, but I'm high
above the town, wrapped in the night's airstreams.
I look down on a puzzle of orange lights
and floodlit squares, the scrabble of roofs,
some frosting hard, some letting out the heat.
The river, a dark scar stitched with bridges, shivers
with reflections. The cathedral's a dazzle. Above it all
I circle and though it's Friday I can't, from here,
make out the girls with bare waists and legs,
rings in their navels, or the lads in thin shirts,
cuffs rolled above wrists as they stride then stagger
from pub to pub. I can't hear the clatter of stilettos,
the cackle of night-out nonsense. A blue light speeds
along the quay but I can't hear the siren I know is there,
on its way to a brawl or broken plate glass
or an anxious group round a prone figure. I can just see
shaded light from a bedroom window and shadows
moving easily like water. But I can't see how
we touch or hear what we say to one another.

Blackspot

You were so taken with your new lover
you drove into the back of Lacey's parked van.
Our car was a right-off.

A fortnight after this I was daydreaming life
with someone else, driving the wagon
with an overhanging load,

when I pulled in to avoid oncoming traffic.
The rear door, tied back illegally,
caught Lacey's shopblind, ripped it off its brackets.

I watched him running for me in the mirror,
apoplectic. When I gave him my name,
our name, he blanched.

We laughed about it later:
the local grocer as inadvertant
blackspot in our blighted lives.

Two years on his business folded and he left home
for an unhappy affair with the chemist's wife.
Somehow we were still together.

Shift

It was time to say goodbye but neither of us moved.
The car might have been a capsule adrift
on the waves, just returned from orbit, not the old
Fiesta we broke down in on holiday last year.

No knock on the hull, no hatch lifting, no
disembodied voice to welcome us back to earth,
just the engine ticking over outside the house
as we sat there recalling the elephant jokes
the AA man told as he fixed the jump leads,
a change from the watertight script
we usually kept to, the technical stuff:
miles per gallon, torque, timing,
double declutching down the gears.

These fortnightly partings were new to us still,
the fine tolerances needed to make it all
work smoothly, the natural shift from men's talk
to a father's arm around a boy's shoulders.

The Wedding Ring

He wouldn't take it off straight away
for fear of courting more bad luck.
Besides, time had worn it into him,
the skin of palm and finger
bulging round its edge the way a tree
grows bark over stapled fence-wire.

But one night, with soap
and a determined twist
he prised it round the knuckle
until it slipped quite naturally
into the bathwater.
He placed it on the window ledge
where it could have been a spare part
the plumber left behind.
Every now and then
he'd rub it on his shirt and wish.

Finally he put it on the back step
and took a hammer to it.
He had imagined
a symbolic shattering of gold fragments,
but instead the soft metal
merely folded clumsily
into an ugly 9 carat lump
he later threw into the river.

For some years a mark remained,
a pale indented band
he'd rub his thumb across absent-mindedly.
And much, much later, gardening
as he grasped the fork shaft
and levered it against the heavy soil,
he'd feel the blister on his palm
just where the mount of skin
used to catch.

The Avalanche

At this hour I'm like an instrument
abandoned so long it's lost its tone. The day
gone shapeless wraps itself round me
like snow. I think of your grandfather, his tale
of mountains so sensitive a cough or a shout
brings the whole place down, buries him
for three days, weightless, breath condensing
to the black fit of an ice-helmet, the first probe
missing by the width of a layer of skin,
atheist's prayers before the second strikes his knee.

Ah, the promises we all make in invisible moments.
No one's looking now. I give you my word on that.
Tinnitus rings a mobile in my head.
If it's you I'll tell you how you've pulled me
from a snowblind hole. Imagine, I'll say,
how your voice must sound
above the tub-thump of a buried heart.

Sir Guy and The Lady Isabella

Side by side we almost touch – shoulder,
elbow, hip; hands in supplication contemplate
the perpendicular, the vaulted light,
the prayer of starlings in the roofspace.
An obedient hounds sleeps at our feet.

All day it's the mumble of tourists,
the verger's cough, footsteps
answering themselves along the nave,
a sermon of unattended thoughts
wittering in the background.

Evenings, the organist crusades against the air.
Then the wooden door creaks;
a shot bolt, turned keys leave us
with the flicker of bats, stutter of candles,
shy beasts of silence grazing stone.

The cold weld between us now
a seam of flesh on a crumpled bed.
As first light picks the lock we're sprawled legs,
a cheek against a shoulder blade,
the scald of skin on skin,
the unleashed hound loping back to join us.

Amicable Numbers

*(Those where the sum of the divisors of one
is equal to the other. The smallest pair of 'friends'
is 220 and 284.)*

The cover drew me,
matt black leather with embossed lettering,
the spine cracked like elm bark,
edges finger-worn and scuffed.
The Encryptor's Companion, Volume One.
A street stall in the Charing Cross Road
the week the Berlin Wall came down.

Inside was a letter,
folded and tucked like a bookmark.
No address. No date. The script,
in claret coloured ink, awkward,
as if wrong-handed. A circle
pencilled round the page number, 220.

Dearest Esther it read *It is important*
to know something about something.
Nabokov knew about butterflies.
I know about nightingales, and a little about cicadas;
their music — malediction with intermissions.
I know nothing of events described by strangers.
Surely it is enough to witness one's life as metaphor.
From the window pollen clouds rise
as the hay is turned. Two buzzards mew and circle
against alchemical blue. Wherever there is roughness
between the fields the nightingale is heard.
But enough. What I ask from you
is not something you might know about.
It is the hint of knowledge passed over,
the hidden current your smile rides
when I look the other way. Yours ever, Jack.

She'll have filed her reply
discreetly I suspect,
nipped in the gutter
so it won't slip out unnoticed.
Volume Two, if I can find it. Page 284.

Your Hand on My Heart

Put your hand on your heart and tell me a tale
I'm bound to believe, quote me figures and facts
so strange and unlikely they have to be real,

how frequencies logged from the song of a whale
speeded up, could be turned into Bacharach hits.
Put your hand on my heart and tell me a tale

of the weight of a feather, the flight of a soul,
the hunter whose dream reveals animal tracks
so strange and unlikely they have to be real.

The map in your head may be scribble and scrawl
but you'll always get home. It's guesswork and wits
and my hand on your heart as you spin me a tale.

I'd go a long way for the charm of your spiel,
though my fingers stay crossed as I step clear of cracks
in the strange and improbable world you make real.

Were we lost out at sea, you could row. I'd bale.
The edge of the world might lurk in the mist,
but your hand on your heart unwinding its tale

would still have me wrapped in the yarn of it all.
Is it true? I might ask. And whatever comes next
my hand on your heart would help me to tell,
though unlikely and strange, this has to be real.

Cauliflower Cheese

Don't speak. Don't interrupt. Whatever
you're bursting to say, save it. This sauce
requires total concentration. Leave
the kitchen to me, unhook the phone.
Take a glass of wine into the garden,
scrutinise the courgettes, their orange trumpets,
inspect the onions, put your nose to the roses,
the ones that smell like pineapple and cream,
laugh at the crossbred primulas, their rings
of clashing colours, worry about white
foxgloves reverting. And the lawn,
yes walk on the lawn, barefoot,
and look over the gate up the valley
to the purple of hills and the winking
early evening lights of Lowgill.

I'll call when it's ready. You can come in then
with all you have to say. But as we face
each other over that brown crust on the sauce,
the sprinkled sesame seeds, buttered mash,
broad beans from the garden, neither
will speak. We'll help each other to seconds,
trying to leave a little for cold, tomorrow.
But we won't. We'll finish the lot.

The Moon Unfinished

Night driving strikes us wordless,
for all there is to tell each other. Dark
hides a smile the other knows is there.
Interference breaks the signal so the News
comes and goes, making less than usual sense.
The moon's a quick curve a painter
might have left, intending to finish later.
Your face in oncoming lights
looks stage-lit, someone I'd be dying to meet
if we hadn't been introduced already.

When we get home I'll open the gate,
knocking the evening's shower
from the weeping cherry, stone-sized drops
soaking my shoulders. Finding you've left
your keys in the kitchen, you'll wait
at the front door, hoping I've got mine.
Once inside, the lights will banish mystery.
I'll look at you and see how much there is
to say still, how much I'll never get round to,
whether or not the painter's finished the moon.

Twins

A curlew bubbles above the evening road.
Sheep turn to stone. Boulders graze the moor.
The wood's edge thickens as I pass.

A figure looms, breaks solitude, speaks like a friend
picking up on an earlier conversation.
He's off to fish, take the night-loch's pulse, talks
of the fox's strategies, the plover chicks he stumbled on
walking a circle to avoid his own trail,
how he knocks on trees to waken owls in daytime.

With a wave he's gone, a shadow among shadows.
Five minutes later though, he's here again, this time
from the opposite direction, a smile of expectation.
The same black moustache, bright fence of teeth,
but instead of the old wax coat and heavy boots
he's wearing shorts and sandals.

And now it's Mozart, Paganini, the favourite hen
he couldn't bear to kill, the plump cat
rolled to a stop on the field's crown,
the cheap bread his neighbour gives
her paying guests, the postman's other round
through the widow's back door every Thursday.

He waves and vanishes again. My footsteps echo
as if I'm being followed. Shadows reach
and touch each other through me.

Brother

I'd be underneath the bedclothes
listening to Journey Into Space.
He'd be out there somewhere,
crossing the Martian desert, come in late
smelling of dark, laugh in the old man's face.

I couldn't swallow meat. I'd pouch my cheeks
with Sunday's roast beef, volunteer
to clear the plates then spit it down the sink.
He'd keep them at the table, talking:
Trade Unions, Gilbert Harding, Hitler.

Going away to school reversed our roles.
He was the one who stayed at home,
kept an eye on things. I'd come back
to find it all the same
and nothing there I wanted anymore.

So I got out early. Put some distance in.
If my parents fretted over anyone it wasn't me.
He went abroad, a wandering figment
I'd make up postcards from, the butt
of funny tales I'd spin my kids.

They're brothers too, both real enough.
And though they now live miles apart
and may, like us, lose touch, at least
each one will know the other could, theoretically,
turn up one day and ask to stay the night.

Stranded

On a scale of 1 to 6 the chiropractor gives her 5,
disc trouble stranding her in San Francisco.
In the crooked mirror the body challenges its image,
youth and grace beseiged by pain.
She can't sit, can barely walk; hobbles,
her e-mails say, to buy an ice-cream,
eats it watching sea-lions bask, slow barges
crease the bay, the fins of white sails
cut the shadow of the bridge, that bridge.

A phone call rides distress, the distant voice
wears a brave face until the question:
What should I do Dad? throws me into panic.
The journey's hers not mine, but suddenly
the fear I'm listening to is mine, not hers.

Before

Before you were serious,
before you bore your share
of the world's weight,
there was a tall leggy girl
with a mouthful of teeth
and wayward hair
her mother despaired of.
She stood with friends
in the shallows of a river,
school tunic tucked into knickers,
splashing the others,
her whole lanky body
throwing itself against the air,
and laughing the sort of laugh
only a chance photo could catch.
She knew if she fell
a friend would be there to hold her
or pick her out of the water
or fall in on top of her even,
screaming with delight.

This was when war
was something that happened
to your parents once,
when your brother was handsome and sane,
when the man you would marry
would look like Clark Gable
and smell like your father,
the son you would have
take after your flattering uncle,
and the woman he would marry
confide in you like a best friend.

Over My Shoulder

Moustaches tusked above a smile, a coy joke
no one gets, a command they do.

Sometimes you're capital A, stiff even at ease,
standing astride the gutter of a dictionary,

a fully paid up literalist, a definition in one;
then again you're a bald man weeping

at Tchaikovsky, a soft-eyed boy at cello lessons,
or a drummer from the days of smooch and swing.

You're a crowd of strangers at the crem,
those curtains closing on the heart,

the taut voice of my mother on the phone,
a distance none of us can measure.

You're those perfectionist's pained eyes
watching me slap emulsion on the wall.

I'm blobs and dribbles, smudged edges,
tight-lipped but all loose ends.

The Long Loss

I lost him overnight, somewhere
between adolescence and the endless
re-adjustments that come next.
I lost him just like that and didn't know it;
miles away, oblivious, trying to get off
with the girl downstairs.
Next morning on the phone
I barely recognised my mother's voice,
hysteria disguised as flatline calm.

I lost him after that
each time my mother cracked
or a man his age shook my hand.
I don't remember where I was
when news broke Kennedy was shot
but I lost him then. Watching newsclips
of the Prague crowds chanting
Dubcek, Svoboda, Dubcek, Svoboda,
I lost him when the tanks rolled in.
And in the Registry I lost him
when my hand shook and my wife
of two whole minutes crossed her fingers.

I lost him in Vietnam, the Fastnet Race,
an earthquake in Japan. I lost him
when my struggling son was born,
small blue-browed apostrophe
bundled in an incubator. I lost him
through a long divorce, decades
of sub-Saharan famine, hostage takers, Aids.
I lost him when his younger sister died,
her eighty-year-old memories worn through.
I lost him so often I lost count:
a misheard voice across the room,
a corny joke, Bing Crosby on the radio.

The House Without Memory

This is the house without memory.

This is the attic with its cobwebs and dust
at the top of the house without memory.

This is the tin trunk, all dents and rust
that sits in the attic of cobwebs and dust
at the top of the house without memory.

This is its key, the only key
and it's locked inside the old tin trunk
great-uncle Joe once huffed and humped
up into the attic and left there to rust
gathering a century's cobwebs and dust
in the house he left without memory.

This is the shadow, uncertain and grey
that falls on the lock whose only key
lies in the trunk still labelled with names,
places like New York, Rangoon and Cannes,
as it sits in the attic and gentilely rusts
under curtains of cobwebs and inches of dust
in the mind of a house without memory.

And this is the skylight that rattles with rain,
veils the moon and filters the sun
that casts the shadow, uncertain and grey
that hides in the night but stoops in the day
like the ghost of aunt Vi picking the lock
to get at the silks and brocades she once packed
along with her dreams in the dented old trunk
left in the attic among cobwebs and junk
in a house that's lost its memory.

And this is the tree that moves in the wind
and flutters the light (as it comes through the pane
that filters the sun and rattles with rain)
so it worries the ghost, uncertain and grey
who can't understand what she's done with the key
and imagines the children she never had
with their terrible need to understand
what lies at the bottom of the battered black tin
that sits under shrouds the spiders have spun
at the top of the house in her memory.

And these are the roots, the roots of the tree
as they push at the stone, crack the cement,
lift the gable an inch so the chimney's bent
like an old man lending an ear to the leaves
that whisper and scatter the light as it moves
to stroke the shadow, uncertain and grey
where she sits on the trunk with a look of dismay
and can't remember what's real and who's died
and what it was she was trying to hide
in the black box whose paintwork is pitted with rust
in the tilting attic of cobwebs and dust
at the top of the house without memory.

Driving Home

I'm all voices, friends I'd lost touch with
remembering one another as they were
before they took off for the four corners.
Stories telescope the years between us.
They say it takes a funeral.

In the rearview mirror the traffic's moving stars.
Two tailgating suns dazzle me. I check
for flashing blue lights, put my foot down.
The tailgater sticks. I pull in,
switch off the engine, wait.

Nothing behind me now but hard shoulder
and a distant constellation coming closer.
By my door a figure stoops.
I wind the window down.
The face we buried earlier today looks in.

The voice, less hesitant than I remember,
still garnished with the chuckle
he'd grant a worn-out joke, announces
I'll give you a ring when I get there.
With an unfamiliar grace he steps away.

A passing wagon slams through where he'd stood.
I drive on slowly, turn the radio loud.
At home they're all in bed. I nurse a whisky,
stretch out on the couch but can't sleep
for the ansaphone's red winking light.

Abstinence

Sex and death: I've done with those
narcotic urges sprung at birth:
a particular skin smell, the way
a tiny muscle in someone's face
moves; a crumbling disc encoded
in the genome, hearing loss or a heart
triggered to self-harm at 54.

Given a chance I'd kick the habit,
renounce flesh for the rough weave
of vows. Whichever deity it is looks down
I'd be there, cross-legged in the street,
not begging alms but dishing out
spells and charms: a traffic-stopping
amulet for jaywalkers, a mantra
for revolving doors, or a small
badge of the Virgin, bodged
and soldered from recycled tin.

I'd scrutinise the crowd, make a sign
I hope you'd recognise and you,
being mortal still, you'd have the edge,
humour me in passing, pass
the time of day as if we'd never lost
that way with language lovers share
trading their fear for their desire.